37164
60. 27

D1303814

ASSESSMENT GUIDE
Grade 3

Harcourt Brace & Company

Orlando • Atlanta • Austin • Boston • San Francisco • Chicago • Dallas • New York •
Toronto • London

Harcourt Brace School Publishers

Contents

Harcourt Brace School Publishers

Overview

In *YOUR HEALTH*, the assessment program, like the instruction, is student-centered. It allows all learners to show what they know and what they can do, thus providing you with ongoing information about each student's understanding of health. Equally important, the assessment program involves the student in self-assessment, offering you strategies for helping students evaluate their own growth.

The *YOUR HEALTH* assessment program is based on the Assessment Model in the chart below. The model's framework shows the multidimensional aspect of the program. The model is balanced between teacher-based and student-based assessments.

The teacher-based strand involves assessments in which the teacher typically evaluates a piece of work as evidence of the student's understanding of the health content and of his or her ability to think critically about it. The teacher-based strand consists of two components: Formal Assessment and Performance Assessment.

The student-based strand of the Assessment Model involves assessments that invite the student to become a partner in the assessment process and to reflect on and evaluate his or her own efforts. The student-based strand also consists of two components: Student Self-Assessment and Portfolio Assessment.

There is a fifth component in the *YOUR HEALTH* assessment program—Daily Assessment. This essential component is listed in the center of the Assessment Model because it is the "glue" that binds together all the other types of assessment.

YOUR HEALTH ASSESSMENT MODEL

PORTFOLIO ASSESSMENT	STUDENT SELF-ASSESSMENT
DAILY ASSESSMENT	
PERFORMANCE ASSESSMENT	FORMAL ASSESSMENT

Description of Assessment Components

Daily Assessment and Classroom Observation

Daily assessment is central to the assessment program. Ultimately, it is the daily events that are observed and recorded that provide the most comprehensive assessment of student growth. *YOUR HEALTH* provides several ways of helping you assess daily student progress.

- *In the Student and Teacher Editions* every lesson ends with a LESSON CHECKUP. These features provide a mix of factual recall, critical thinking, and skill questions.
- *In this Assessment Guide* a Life Skills Observation Checklist (page 6) can help you evaluate students' skills in health.

Student Self-Assessment

Student Self-Assessment encourages students to reflect on and monitor their own gains in health knowledge, development of life skills, and changes in attitude.

- *In the Student and Teacher Editions* Journal Notes, Set Health Goals, and Use Life Skills are features of every chapter. These features encourage students to reflect on what they have learned and apply their new knowledge to their lives.
- *In this Assessment Guide* you will find a Healthy Habits Checklist (page 8) for students to use in assessing their current level of wellness. The Individual Self-Assessment Checklist (page 9) and the Team Self-Assessment Checklist (page 10) can be used to aid students in reflecting on their performance.

Portfolio Assessment

Students make their own portfolios in Portfolio Assessment. Portfolios may also contain a few required or teacher-selected papers.

- *In the Student and Teacher Editions* every chapter includes a wealth of activities that results in products that can be included as portfolio items.
- *In this Assessment Guide* are support materials (pages 11–15) to assist you and your students in developing portfolios and in using them to evaluate growth in health.

Formal Assessment

Formal assessments can help you reinforce and assess students' understandings of ideas developed in each chapter. Chapter Reviews and Tests require students to reflect on, summarize, and apply chapter concepts.

- *In the Student and Teacher Editions* each chapter ends with a chapter review and test.
- *In this Assessment Guide* is a test for each chapter (beginning on page 18). Answers are shown in reduced form in the Teacher Edition, as well as in the Answer Key on pages 54–62.

Performance Assessment

Health literacy involves more than just what students know. It is also concerned with how they think and how they do things. The Chapter Project is a performance task that can provide you with insights about students' knowledge, skills, and behaviors.

- *In the Student and Teacher Editions* a project is described on each chapter opening page. Periodically throughout each chapter, Project Check-Up tips provide strategies for encouraging students to continue working on their projects. Projects are assessed at the ends of chapters.
- *In this Assessment Guide* a scoring rubric for each project is provided following each Chapter Test. Students can assess their own performance on a project using the Student Project Summary Sheet found on page 17.

DAILY ASSESSMENT and CLASSROOM OBSERVATION

In *YOUR HEALTH,* "child watching" is a natural and continual part of teaching and an important part of the evaluation process. The purpose is to record observations that can lead to improved instruction in health. An observation checklist is provided on page 6 for recording student performance on six life skills that are emphasized in *YOUR HEALTH.* These skills are listed and described below. Indicators to help you evaluate each skill appear on the checklist.

❑ **Make Decisions**—the process of selecting among alternatives to decide the wisest thing to do in order to avoid risky situations or health risks.

❑ **Refuse**—selecting and using strategies to effectively react to peer pressure so as to avoid a risky action.

❑ **Resolve Conflicts**—selecting and using strategies to effectively communicate and compromise in order to find solutions to problems or to avoid violence.

❑ **Manage Stress**—acting to relieve the symptoms of stress that occur when physical, intellectual, emotional, or social needs are not met.

❑ **Communicate**—using strategies to transmit information, ideas, needs, feelings or requests in a form that aids interpretation.

❑ **Set Goals**—deciding what improvements to make in one's physical, intellectual, social, or emotional condition and taking action to move toward those goals.

Tips for Using
Life Skills Observation Checklist

- Survey the Chapter Organizer, the margin features, and the Chapter Review pages in your Teacher's Edition to identify the life skills developed in a chapter. Then decide which of these features you wish to assess using the checklist.

- Select several students to observe. Often your observations can be more effective if you focus your attention on only a few students rather than trying to observe the whole class at once.

- Don't agonize over the ratings. Students who stand out as particularly strong will clearly merit a rating of 3. Others will clearly earn a rating of 1. This doesn't mean, however, that a 2 is automatically the appropriate rating for the rest of the class. There may be students who have not had sufficient opportunity to display their strengths or weaknesses. In those instances, Not Enough Opportunity to Observe may be the most appropriate rating.

- Use the data you collect. Refer to your observation checklist while making lesson plans, evaluating your students' growth in health, constructing cooperative learning groups, and holding conferences with students and family members.

Life Skills Observation Checklist

Students' Names

✔ Make Decisions

Skill Indicators: The student

- considers options, risks, and constraints
- role-plays healthful decision making
- makes wise decisions in everyday situations

✔ Refuse

Skill Indicators: The student

- says *no* in a convincing way
- suggests healthful alternatives to health-risking activities
- uses facts to explain reasons for refusal
- walks away if peer pressure becomes too great

✔ Resolve Conflicts

Skill Indicators: The student

- explores options
- listens attentively to others
- deals with a problem calmly or makes plans to discuss the problem at a later time
- walks away if a situation may become violent

✔ Manage Stress

Skill Indicators: The student

- analyzes the cause of the stress
- talks over feelings and seeks help if necessary
- finds an outlet, such as exercise

✔ Communicate

Skill Indicators: The student

- seeks help for problems
- presents ideas clearly
- fulfills the purpose of the communication
- listens attentively to others

✔ Set Goals

Skill Indicators: The student

- sets reasonable goals to improve or maintain health
- makes an action plan to achieve goals
- is disciplined in following a plan
- evaluates the results of personal efforts

Harcourt Brace School Publishers

STUDENT SELF-ASSESSMENT

Researchers have evidence that self-assessment and the reflection it involves can have significant and positive effects on learning. To achieve these effects, students must be challenged to reflect on their work and to monitor, analyze, and control their own learning—beginning in the earliest grades.

Your Health provides three checklists to encourage self-assessment.

- The "Healthy Habits Checklist" allows each student to do a self-assessment of his or her level of wellness. The checklist helps students target health areas to work on throughout the year.
- The "My Thoughts Exactly!" checklist allows individual students to reflect on their work at the end of a chapter.
- The "How Did Your Team Do?" checklist provides an opportunity for a team of students to reflect on how they did after they have worked cooperatively on a health activity or project.

Other opportunities for student self-assessment include Journal Notes and the Set Health Goals and Use Life Skills questions found at the end of each lesson. Note that Journal Notes provide an opportunity for private self-assessment and reflection and should not be used for evaluation or assessment.

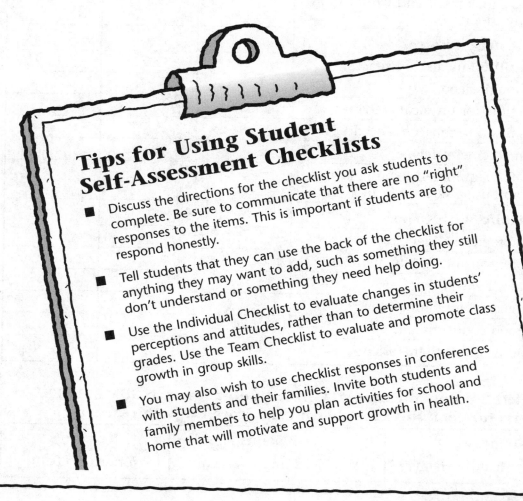

Tips for Using Student Self-Assessment Checklists

- Discuss the directions for the checklist you ask students to complete. Be sure to communicate that there are no "right" responses to the items. This is important if students are to respond honestly.

- Tell students that they can use the back of the checklist for anything they may want to add, such as something they still don't understand or something they need help doing.

- Use the Individual Checklist to evaluate changes in students' perceptions and attitudes, rather than to determine their grades. Use the Team Checklist to evaluate and promote class growth in group skills.

- You may also wish to use checklist responses in conferences with students and their families. Invite both students and family members to help you plan activities for school and home that will motivate and support growth in health.

Name _____ Date _____

Chapter Title _____

Healthy Habits Checklist

This quiz will tell you how healthy your daily habits are. Put a check-mark in the proper column. When finished, add up your score. Take the quiz several times this year and see how your health habits improve!

	ALWAYS	SOMETIMES	NEVER
Using Life Skills			
1. I weigh options and make healthful decisions.			
2. I say *no* if I need to.			
3. I resolve conflicts peacefully.			
4. I use stress-management strategies.			
5. I communicate with others clearly.			
6. I set goals for myself and work toward attaining them.			
Making Healthy Choices			
1. I eat healthful meals and snacks.			
2. I get enough sleep.			
3. I make time for physical activities.			
4. I avoid alcohol, tobacco, and drugs.			
5. I take medicines safely.			
6. I use safety equipment when playing sports and use a safety belt in a car.			
Getting Along with Others			
1. I have some close friends.			
2. I am a responsible family member.			
3. I work well with others.			
4. I apologize when I am wrong.			
5. I feel good about myself.			
6. I get along with other students.			

Give yourself 2 points for each ALWAYS, 1 point for each SOMETIMES, and 0 points for each NEVER. Add up your score for each category.

8-12 points	4-7 points	0-6 points
You Have Healthy Habits!	You Need Improvement	Work to Do Better

Name _____ Date _____

Chapter Title _____

My Thoughts Exactly!

Decide whether you agree or disagree with each statement below. Circle the word that tells what you think. If you are not sure, circle the question mark. Use the back of the sheet for comments.

1. I understand the ideas in this chapter.   Agree   ?   Disagree

2. I found this chapter interesting.   Agree   ?   Disagree

3. I learned a lot.   Agree   ?   Disagree

4. I liked working as a member of a group
    better than working alone on activities.   Agree   ?   Disagree

5. I contributed my share of work to group
    activities.   Agree   ?   Disagree

6. I helped others at home and at school.   Agree   ?   Disagree

7. I am getting better at decision making.   Agree   ?   Disagree

8. I make my needs, feelings, and ideas
    known to my family, friends, and others.   Agree   ?   Disagree

9. I focus more on my strengths than my
    weaknesses.   Agree   ?   Disagree

10. I practice good health habits.   Agree   ?   Disagree

Think about each question below and write a short answer to each one.

11. What did you like best in this chapter? Tell why. _____

_____

_____

12. What would you like to learn more about? _____

_____

_____

How Did Your Team Do?

Read each item. Mark the number that tells the score you think your team deserves.

How well did your team	High		Low
1. plan for the activity?	3	2	1
2. carry out team plans?	3	2	1
3. listen to and show respect for each member?	3	2	1
4. share the work?	3	2	1
5. make decisions and solve problems?	3	2	1
6. make use of available resources?	3	2	1
7. organize information?	3	2	1
8. communicate what was learned?	3	2	1

Review your answers to 1 through 8. Then answer the questions below.

9. What did your team do best? _____

_____

_____

10. What can you do to help your team do better work?

_____

_____

11. What did your team like most about the activity?

_____

_____

PORTFOLIO ASSESSMENT

For portfolio assessment, students make collections of their work. Their portfolios may include a few required papers such as the Project Summary Sheet, Project Evaluation Sheet, and Individual Self-Assessment Checklist. Beyond these, students have the opportunity to add work samples that they believe represent their growth in health.

Portfolios
- **provide comprehensive pictures of student progress.**
- **foster reflection, self-monitoring, and self-assessment.**

The value of portfolios is in making them and in discussing them, not in the collection content itself. Organizers are provided on the following pages to help you and your students make and use them for evaluation.

Getting Started with Portfolio Assessment

- Introduce portfolios by explaining that artists, fashion designers, writers, and other people use portfolios to present samples of their best work when they are applying for jobs. Explain that the purpose of student portfolios is to show samples of their work in health.

- Engage your students in a discussion of the kinds of work samples they might choose and the reasons for their choices. For example, the portfolio might include a written work sample, Activity Book pages, and a creative product. Point out that students' best work is not necessarily their longest or their neatest. Discuss reasons for also including a few standard pieces in each portfolio, and decide what those pieces should be. The Project Summary Sheet (page 17), for example, might be a standard piece in all portfolios because it shows the student's ability to use knowledge and skills to solve a problem.

■ Another standard portfolio piece might be the Health Experiences Record (page 13), on which students log their independent health activities, including out-of-school experiences related to health. The Health Experiences Record can reveal student interests and ideas you might otherwise not know about.

■ Establish a basic plan that shows how many work samples will be included in the portfolio, what they will be, and when they should be selected. Ask students to list on A Guide to My Health Portfolio (page 14) each sample they select and explain why they selected it.

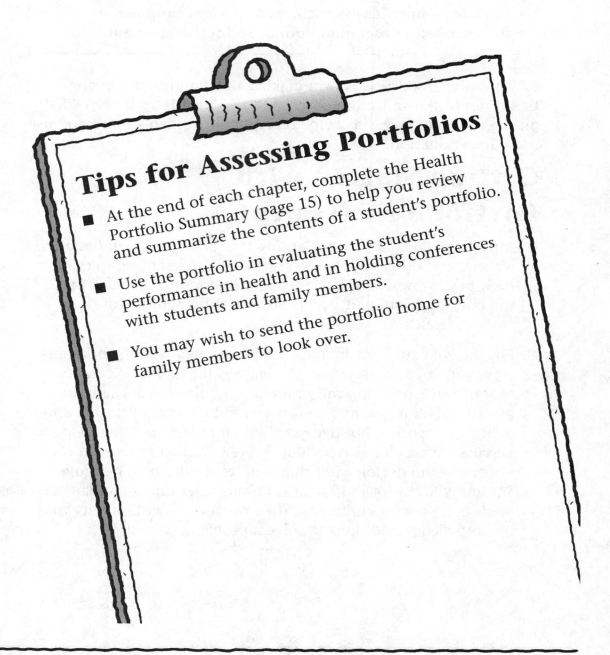

Tips for Assessing Portfolios

■ At the end of each chapter, complete the Health Portfolio Summary (page 15) to help you review and summarize the contents of a student's portfolio.

■ Use the portfolio in evaluating the student's performance in health and in holding conferences with students and family members.

■ You may wish to send the portfolio home for family members to look over.

Name _____

Health Experiences Record

Date	What I Did	What I Thought or Learned

Name _____ Date _____

A Guide to My Health Portfolio

What Is In My Portfolio	Why I Chose It
1.	
2.	
3.	
4.	
5.	
6.	
7.	
8.	

I organized my portfolio this way because _____

_____

_____

_____

_____

Harcourt Brace School Publishers

Date _____

Goals	Evidence and Comments
1. Growth in knowledge about health and safety.	
2. Growth in using life skills: • make decisions • refuse • resolve conflicts • manage stress • communicate • set goals	
3. Growth in ability to locate, gather, organize, and communicate information about health.	
4. Growth in ability to practice good health habits.	

SUMMARY OF PORTFOLIO ASSESSMENT

FOR THIS REVIEW			SINCE LAST REVIEW		
Excellent	**Good**	**Fair**	**Improving**	**The Same**	**Not as Good**

CHAPTER TESTS AND PROJECTS

Using Chapter Tests

The Chapter Tests can help you find out how well your students understand, integrate, and apply the important ideas that are developed in each chapter. Included in each test are numerous thought-provoking items that require the student to reflect on and summarize chapter ideas, rather than simply to recall them.

You will find answers to the chapter tests in the Answer Key of this Assessment Guide as well as in reduced form at the end of each chapter in the Teacher Edition.

Follow-up discussion of students' responses to test items is encouraged. Discussion gives students the opportunity to explain their answers. (Creative students may devise an unforeseen solution to a problem or apply concepts in a correct but unexpected manner.) Discussion also helps dispel any lingering misconceptions students may have about the topic.

Using Projects as Performance Assessments

The Chapter Project is a performance task that can provide you with insights about students' understandings, skills, behaviors, and attitudes about health. The project also requires the use of skills such as critical thinking, decision making, and problem solving. You can use the project to evaluate the performance of both individuals and teams.

You may want to read the teacher suggestions for introducing the project a few days before students begin to work on it. Suggestions are in each Introduce the Chapter part of your Teacher Edition.

Before students begin the project, explain how you will evaluate their performance. You may want to use the scoring rubric provided for each project. (See the Project Evaluation Sheet that follows each Chapter Test in this guide.) If so, explain the three-point scoring system in language students can understand.

Distribute and discuss the Project Summary Sheet provided on the following page. You may wish to have students complete this sheet as they work on the project or after they finish it.

To Sum It Up

You can tell about your project by completing the following sentences.

1. My project was about _____
   _____
   _____

2. I worked on this project with _____
   _____
   _____

3. I gathered information from these sources: _____
   _____
   _____

4. The most important thing I learned from doing this project is _____
   _____
   _____

5. I am going to use what I have learned by _____
   _____
   _____

6. I'd also like to tell you _____
   _____
   _____

Harcourt Brace School Publishers

"About Myself and Others"

Write *T* or *F* to show if the sentence is true or false.

_____ **1.** If you respect yourself, you believe in yourself.

_____ **2.** Being responsible means that others cannot count on you.

_____ **3.** Being honest means to tell the truth.

_____ **4.** One way we show feelings is through words.

_____ **5.** No one shows feelings through actions.

_____ **6.** Body language helps us show our feelings to others.

_____ **7.** Emotions are strong feelings that few people have.

_____ **8.** When we have self-control, we cannot control our unpleasant feelings.

_____ **9.** One way of letting go of emotions is by forgiving yourself or others for what happened.

_____ **10.** There is no one else in the whole world just like you.

Match a strong emotion listed below with the story that best describes what that person is feeling. Write the name of the emotion on the line at the left.

fear	stress
grief	anger

_____ **11.** Beth is not speaking to her best friend, Toni, because Toni is telling lies about Beth. Beth found out about the lies, and doesn't want to be friends with Toni anymore.

_____ **12.** Pedro plays alone in his yard most days after school. Sometimes the neighbor's dog runs over to him, barking and growling. Pedro doesn't like this dog, and wishes that his neighbor would keep it tied up.

_____ **13.** Lauren's teacher told her class about an important spelling test coming up at the end of the week. Lauren forgot about it, and now it's the night before the big test. Lauren is not a good speller, and should have been studying the spelling list all week. She is very worried about the test.

_____ **14.** Jaime's cat was 18 years old and had been sick for awhile. The medicine the veterinarian gave the sick cat no longer worked. The cat died last night. Jaime loved his cat very much.

15. Name one time when you should ask for help.

_____

_____

_____

_____

16. Name one good way of dealing with stress.

_____

_____

17. Name one step to take to help manage anger.

_____

_____

_____

18. Draw a picture that shows you and a friend using good communication skills.

19. Draw a picture that shows what it means to have compassion.

Name _____ Date _____

Write the letter of the best answer on the line at the
left to complete the sentence.

_____ **20.** When you have good relationships with your family and friends, it
makes you _____ .
a. feel good about yourself   b. get better grades in school
c. make more friends   d. feel bad about yourself

_____ **21.** Families work together better when family members _____ .
a. do their own thing   b. have lots of arguments
c. respect and trust each other d. own lots of things

_____ **22.** When you and a friend disagree, you should _____ .
a. never speak to each other again
b. try to listen and talk things over
c. find a new friend
d. say mean things and walk away

_____ **23.** When friends want you to do something just because "everyone is
doing it," they are using _____ .
a. peer pressure   b. peer teasing
c. peer example   d. peer fun

_____ **24.** If you have compassion, you _____ .
a. have a disease   b. dislike most people
c. think only of yourself   d. can feel what others feel

25. Write an "I-message" about how you feel when someone in your family
hurts your feelings.

_____

_____

_____

_____

_____

Chapter Project Evaluation Sheet (Teacher)

**Rubric for Evaluating Student Performance
on the Chapter 1 Project**

Project: Draw pictures of and act out emotions

Purpose: To gather and organize information about emotions; to develop work skills; to use what is learned from the project in everyday life

Use the indicators below to help you determine the student's overall score.

Level 3
The student fulfills the purpose of the project in an exemplary way.

_____ Organizes information from a variety of sources

_____ Draws pictures that show a range of at least four emotions

_____ Acts out how these four emotions feel

_____ Works cooperatively with a partner

_____ Communicates ideas clearly and effectively through drawings and actions

_____ Demonstrates strong commitment to using information from this project to understand and control his or her own emotions

Level 2
The student fulfills the purpose of the project in a satisfactory way.

_____ Organizes information from more than one source

_____ Draws pictures that show a range of at least two emotions

_____ Acts out how these two emotions feel

_____ Works cooperatively with a partner most of the time

_____ Communicates ideas reasonably well through drawings and actions

_____ Demonstrates some commitment to using information from this project to understand and control his or her own emotions

Level 1
The student does not fulfill the purpose of the project.

_____ Gathers insufficient information or uses only one source

_____ Fails to draw pictures that show at least two emotions

_____ Fails to act out how at least two emotions feel

_____ Fails to work cooperatively with a partner

_____ Has difficulty communicating ideas through drawings and actions

_____ Demonstrates little commitment to using information from this project to understand and control his or her own emotions

Student's overall score _____

Teacher comments:

Name _____ Date _____

"Me and My Family"

Write *T* or *F* to show if the sentence is true or false.

_____ 1. A family is a group of people you work with or go to school with.

_____ 2. Your family makes sure your basic needs are met.

_____ 3. Families also teach values.

_____ 4. Values are strong teachings about how to cheat other people.

_____ 5. All families look the same.

_____ 6. Every family member has responsibilities.

_____ 7. You are being responsible when you do a job without waiting to be asked.

_____ 8. Playing together as a family helps make everyone happy.

_____ 9. Respecting family members is not an important thing to do.

_____ 10. Children first learn about right and wrong in their families.

Choose the best words from the word bank to complete the story below.

| family rules | changes | family | divorce |
| communicate | remarriage | sibling | |

The Boyle family is going through some hard **11.** _____.

Mr. and Mrs. Boyle are getting a **12.** _____. They are worried about their children. Patrick is nine years old, and he has one

13. _____, who is four years old. Mr. and Mrs. Boyle try to

14. _____ often with their children. They want the children to

know that they will always be a **15.** _____ even when big changes like this one happen.

Name _____ Date _____

Match the facts about the human life cycle with
the correct stages of growth. Write the letter of
the sentences on the lines at the left.

_____ **16.** Birth to Two   _____ **17.** Two to Ten

_____ **18.** Ten to Adult   _____ **19.** Adult to Senior

a. During this stage, a person grows at an amazing rate.

b. During this stage, a person decides whether or not to get married.

c. During this stage, a person's language skills develop quickly. The person
can do complex tasks, such as riding a bicycle.

d. During this stage, a person changes from a child into an adult.

20. List three ways in which you have changed since you were a baby.

_____

_____

_____

Write the letter of the best answer on the line at
the left.

_____ **21.** What is the smallest working part of your body?
    a. skin   **b.** cell   **c.** blood   **d.** organ

_____ **22.** Cells that are long and thin and carry signals through your body
are called _____ cells.
    a. bone   **b.** heart   **c.** skin   **d.** nerve

_____ **23.** Cells that work together to get a job done are called _____.
    a. tissues   **b.** bone cells   **c.** organs   **d.** nerve cells

_____ **24.** Groups of tissues join together to form _____.
    a. organ   **b.** tissues   **c.** organs   **d.** muscles
    systems

_____ **25.** Your growth rate is _____.
    a. how quickly you become   **b.** how slow you are at
      an adult   learning new things
    c. how quickly or slowly   **d.** how you grew as a baby
      you grow

26. Jose is worried about how he is growing. His twin sister is already four inches taller than he is. He is worried that his body might not be growing as it should. What could you tell Jose to help him feel better about his growth rate?

_____

_____

_____

_____

27. Name three good health habits you and your classmates could practice to make sure your bodies stay healthy and grow strong.

_____

_____

_____

_____

28. Sue Ann doesn't like the way an adult member of her family touches her. What should she do?

_____

_____

_____

_____

29. What is wrong with comparing yourself to other people your age?

_____

_____

_____

_____

30. Name the parts of your body that work together to make up the circulatory system.

_____

_____

_____

Harcourt Brace School Publishers

Name _____ Date _____

Chapter Project Evaluation Sheet (Teacher)

Rubric for Evaluating Student Performance on the Chapter 2 Project

Project: Make a family book
Purpose: To gather and organize information about the skills and responsibilities of the members of the family; to develop work skills; to use what is learned from the project in everyday life

Use the indicators below to help you determine the student's overall score.

Level 3
The student fulfills the purpose of the project in an exemplary way.

_____ Gathers information by interviewing each family member

_____ Organizes information to demonstrate a thorough understanding of the skills and responsibilities of each family member

_____ Works alone with initiative or works cooperatively with others

_____ Communicates ideas clearly and effectively through a family book

_____ Demonstrates strong ability to apply what was learned

Level 2
The student fulfills the purpose of the project in a satisfactory way.

_____ Gathers information by interviewing more than one family member

_____ Organizes information to demonstrate a reasonable understanding of the skills and responsibilities of each family member

_____ Works alone with initiative or works cooperatively with others much of the time

_____ Communicates in a reasonably clear and effective way through a family book

_____ Demonstrates some ability to apply what was learned

Level 1
The student does not fulfill the purpose of the project.

_____ Gathers insufficient information or interviews only one family member

_____ Fails to organize information to demonstrate adequate understanding of the skills and responsibilities of each family member

_____ Lacks initiative when working alone or fails to work cooperatively

_____ Has difficulty communicating clear, complete ideas in a booklet

_____ Fails to demonstrate ability to apply what was learned

Student's overall score _____
Teacher comments:

Keeping My Body Fit

Write *T* or *F* to show if the sentence is true or false.

_____ **1.** Tiny holes in your skin are called pores.

_____ **2.** Sweat helps warm your body.

_____ **3.** Bacteria are living things that are so tiny you cannot see them.

_____ **4.** Some bacteria cause illness.

_____ **5.** Washing one's hands often is an important way of stopping the spread of illnesses.

_____ **6.** You need protection from the sun only if your skin does not tan.

_____ **7.** The sun is strongest in the middle of the day.

_____ **8.** Sunscreen does not protect you from the sun's harmful rays.

_____ **9.** Only your skin needs protection from the sun.

_____ **10.** Never look right at the sun, even if you're wearing sunglasses.

Use the words below to fill in the blanks.

mouth guard	cavity	fluoride
dental floss	plaque	

Ben had an appointment with the dentist. The last time that Ben went to the dentist, the dentist reminded him to brush his teeth twice a day with a

toothpaste that has **11.** _____ and to use

12. _____ once a day. The dentist said that by doing these two things every day, Ben could reduce the amount of

13. _____ on his teeth. Ben also learned that it was

important for him to wear a **14.** _____ when he played soccer. When the dentist finished examining Ben's teeth, he told Ben that he was doing a great job of caring for his teeth. Ben did not have a single

15. _____! Ben was very glad that he had done all the things the dentist had told him to do.

Look carefully at the diagram below. Then label each part of the ear. Use the words below to help you.

| ear canal | eardrum | middle ear |
| inner ear | outer ear | |

16. _____

17. _____

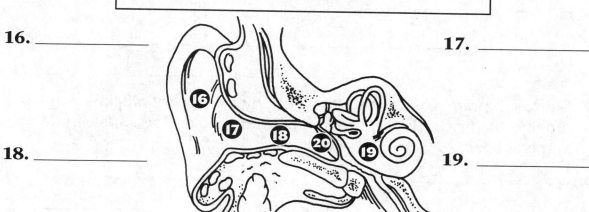

18. _____

19. _____

20. _____

21. Susan plays baseball. She wants to protect her ears while she's playing this game. What could she do? _____

22. Mike sometimes gets nosebleeds. When he gets a nosebleed, he tips his head backward. What is Mike doing wrong? _____

_____

_____

Write the letter of the best answer on the line at the left.

_____ 23. Any activity that makes your body work hard is called ____ .
    a. stretching   b. exercising
    c. strengthening   d. aerobic exercise

_____ 24. This kind of exercise speeds up your heart and breathing and helps your whole body work better.
    a. warm-up exercise   b. cool-down exercise
    c. stretching exercise   d. aerobic exercise

_____ **25.** Rest is important because it helps your muscles _____ .
         a. relax   **b.** stretch
         c. become more flexible   **d.** work better

26. Kenny woke up late for soccer practice. He hurried over to the field to meet his coach and teammates. Kenny went straight out on the field and started playing. He soon got a bad cramp in his leg muscles. What did Kenny forget to do before playing?

_____

_____

27. Marta felt pain in her ankle when her physical education class was running the track. She kept running. What should Marta have done immediately?

_____

_____

28. Brad and Ted went bike riding together. They rode for three hours and were very tired when they got home. The boys got off their bikes and sat on Brad's front steps for an hour. When they tried to stand up, their leg muscles were very stiff and sore. What did the boys forget to do after bike riding?

_____

_____

29. Meg fell and broke her arm. She now has the cast off but she is having trouble using her arm. Her mother took her to a physical therapist. What kind of help will the physical therapist give Meg?

_____

_____

30. Louis twisted his knee while playing football with his friends. His friends took him home. Louis's dad knew what to do to help Louis's sprained knee. What did Louis's dad do?

_____

_____

Name _____ Date _____

Chapter Project Evaluation Sheet (Teacher)

Rubric for Evaluating Student Performance on the Chapter 3 Project

Project: Plan an exercise game
Purpose: To gather and organize information about an exercise; to develop work skills; to use what is learned from the project in everyday life

Use the indicators below to help you determine the student's overall score.

Level 3
The student fulfills the purpose of the project in an exemplary way.

_____ Organizes a game that demonstrates a thorough understanding of all the elements of a good exercise program

_____ Discusses the game thoroughly with a health professional (or teacher)

_____ Works alone with initiative or works cooperatively with others

_____ Communicates clearly and effectively

_____ Demonstrates strong commitment to applying the information to own life

Level 2

The student fulfills the purpose of the project in a satisfactory way.

_____ Organizes a game that demonstrates a reasonable understanding of all the elements of a good exercise program

_____ Discusses the game to some extent with a health professional (or teacher)

_____ Works alone with initiative or cooperatively with others most of the time

_____ Communicates in a reasonably clear and effective way

_____ Demonstrates some commitment to applying the information to own life

Level 1

The student does not fulfill the purpose of the project.

_____ Fails to organize a game that demonstrates a reasonable understanding of all the elements of a good exercise program

_____ Fails to discuss the game with a health professional (or teacher)

_____ Fails to use initiative when working alone or to cooperate with others

_____ Has difficulty communicating ideas

_____ Demonstrates little commitment to applying the information to own life

Student's overall score _____

Teacher comments:

Food for a Healthy Body

Write the letter of the correct answer on the line at the left.

_____ **1.** What do we call the parts of food that help your body grow and get energy?
    a. fiber   **b.** servings   **c.** nutrients   **d.** grains

_____ **2.** What do we call the foods a person usually eats and drinks?
    a. diet   **b.** nutrients   **c.** vegetables   **d.** fiber

_____ **3.** What do we call the part of some foods that helps keep food moving through the intestines?
    a. proteins   **b.** fiber   **c.** nutrients   **d.** vitamins

_____ **4.** What do we call the study of food and how it affects the body?
    a. science   **b.** energy   **c.** education   **d.** nutrition

_____ **5.** Which foods below come from plants?
    a. milk and dairy products   **b.** meat and fish
    c. grains, nuts, and beans   **d.** eggs

Write *T* or *F* to show if the sentence is true or false.

_____ **6.** A spoiled food is one that is unsafe to eat.

_____ **7.** You should store foods such as milk and meat in the refrigerator.

_____ **8.** You should always store leftovers in the cupboard.

_____ **9.** Pathogens don't cause illness.

_____ **10.** Germs is another name for pathogens.

_____ **11.** You should chop fruit on a cutting board you just used for meat.

_____ **12.** Wrapping foods keeps out air and pathogens.

_____ **13.** Washing your hands helps to keep pathogens off your food.

_____ **14.** Frozen foods can also be kept in the refrigerator.

_____ **15.** Pathogens don't spread from one food to another.

Name _____ Date _____

Look carefully at the Food Guide Pyramid. Then write
the name of each food group on the line.
The top food group is done for you.

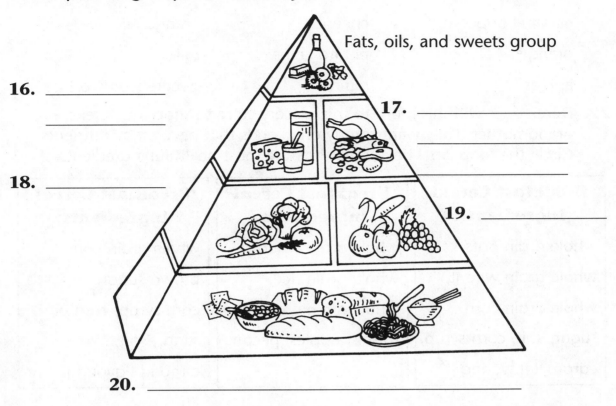

Fats, oils, and sweets group

16. _____
    _____

17. _____
    _____

18. _____

19. _____

20. _____

21. From which food group should we have the most servings each day?

_____

22. From which food group should we have the fewest servings each day?

_____

23. What beverage should we drink six to eight glasses of each day?

_____

24. When we eat foods from each of the food groups every day, what kind
    of a diet do we have?

_____

25. Should we eat all of our daily food at one time of the day? Why or
    why not?

_____

26. Brad and Brenda want a healthful after-school snack. Circle the snacks listed below that would be their best choices. (7)

candy	bagels	cookies
caramel popcorn	cheese	orange juice
oranges	potato chips	milk
apples	raisins	sweetened cereal

27. Derek goes with his mom to the grocery store to shop for Derek's grandmother. They want to buy only foods that have many nutrients. Circle the food label below that lists the most healthful ingredients.

Breakfast Cereal Ingredients:	**Breakfast Cereal Ingredients:**	**Breakfast Cereal Ingredients:**
whole grain oats, whole grain wheat, whole grain corn, sugar, salt, corn syrup, caramel flavoring	whole grain wheat, whole grain rice, whole grain corn, raisins, apples, pecans	whole grain corn, brown sugar, corn syrup, corn oil, sugar, salt, almond flavoring

In each of the following pairs of food, circle the choice that probably offers the best value.

28. a large can of orange juice
a package of three individual containers of juice with straws

29. Super-Duper Whole Wheat Crackers
Store Brand Whole Wheat Crackers

30. a large bag of pretzels
small bags of pretzels with only one serving in each

Name _____ Date _____

Chapter Project Evaluation Sheet (Teacher)

**Rubric for Evaluating Student Performance
on the Chapter 4 Project**

Project: Make a food display
Purpose: To gather and organize information to show balanced meals; to develop work
          skills; to use what is learned from the project in everyday life

Use the indicators below to help you determine the student's overall score.

Level 3
The student fulfills the purpose of the project in an exemplary way.

_____ Gathers information from a variety of sources

_____ Organizes information to demonstrate a thorough understanding of a
        balanced meal

_____ Works alone with initiative or works cooperatively with others

_____ Communicates ideas clearly and effectively through a food display

_____ Demonstrates strong ability to apply the information in the food display to a
        personal commitment to eating balanced meals

Level 2
The student fulfills the purpose of the project in a satisfactory way.

_____ Gathers information from more than one source

_____ Organizes information to demonstrate a reasonable understanding of a
        balanced meal

_____ Works alone with initiative or works cooperatively with others most of the time

_____ Communicates ideas through a food display in a reasonably clear and
        effective way

_____ Demonstrates some ability to apply the information in the food display to a
        personal commitment to eating balanced meals

Level 1
The student does not fulfill the purpose of the project.

_____ Gathers insufficient information or uses only one source

_____ Fails to organize information to demonstrate an adequate understanding of a
        balanced meal

_____ Lacks initiative when working alone or fails to work cooperatively

_____ Has difficulty communicating clear, complete ideas through a food display

_____ Demonstrates little ability to apply the information in the food display to a
        personal commitment to eating balanced meals

Student's overall score _____
Teacher comments:

Preventing Disease

Match the words about disease and its causes with their definitions. Write the letter of the correct answer on the line at the left of the definition.

_____ **1.** a body temperature that is higher than normal

_____ **2.** very simple living things that can cause infectious diseases such as strep throat

_____ **3.** a sign that something is wrong in the body

_____ **4.** a liquid, powder, cream, spray, or pill used to treat illness

_____ **5.** germs that cause disease

_____ **6.** when a pathogen that causes disease cannot make a person ill

_____ **7.** a substance given that keeps you from getting an illness

_____ **8.** one of the tiniest pathogens that causes disease such as the common cold

_____ **9.** something that causes the body not to work normally

_____ **10.** a disease that can spread from one person to another

a. symptom

b. disease

c. infectious disease

d. pathogens

e. bacteria

f. virus

g. fever

h. immune

i. vaccine

j. medicine

Name _____ Date _____

Write *T* or *F* to show if the sentence is true or false.

_____ **11.** A cold is an infectious disease.

_____ **12.** Allergies can be spread from one person to another.

_____ **13.** Bacteria are found only in the air.

_____ **14.** Not all bacteria cause disease.

_____ **15.** It is okay for children to take medicine all by themselves.

_____ **16.** Noninfectious diseases can be caught from or spread to other people.

_____ **17.** During an asthma attack, airways in the lungs become narrow.

_____ **18.** Our body cells use sugar to make energy.

_____ **19.** A doctor uses a tongue depressor to find out if someone has diabetes.

_____ **20.** Diabetes is an infectious disease.

Use what you know about noninfectious diseases to answer the following questions.

21. Alicia has allergies. She is allergic to dogs and cats. What can Alicia's doctor do for her to help her live more comfortably with her allergies?

_____

_____

22. Kenny has asthma. When he has an asthma attack, it is hard for him to breathe. What might make Kenny have an asthma attack?

_____

_____

_____

23. James's mother has diabetes. She learned that there are two things she can do to help control this disease. What are they?

_____

_____

Harcourt Brace School Publishers

24. Read the lunch menus below. Draw a circle around the lunch menu
that would be the healthier choice.

Menu #1	Menu #2
spaghetti with sauce	cheeseburger
fresh green salad	French fries
apple	large soft drink
cup of milk	candy bar

25. Lena doesn't believe exercise is important. She spends most of her time
watching TV and playing video games. What two reasons could you
give Lena for exercising every day?

Reason 1: _____

_____

Reason 2: _____

_____

Harcourt Brace School Publishers

Chapter Project Evaluation Sheet (Teacher)

Rubric for Evaluating Student Performance
on the Chapter 5 Project

Project: Make bulletin board about how to avoid germs

Purpose: To gather and organize information about the spread of germs; to develop work skills; to use what is learned from the project in everyday life

Use the indicators below to help you determine the student's overall score.

Level 3
The student fulfills the purpose of the project in an exemplary way.

_____ Gathers information from a variety of sources

_____ Organizes information to demonstrate a thorough understanding of how germs are spread and how people can stop the spread of germs

_____ Works alone with initiative or works cooperatively with others

_____ Communicates ideas clearly and effectively through a bulletin board display

_____ Demonstrates strong commitment to stop the spread of germs

Level 2
The student fulfills the purpose of the project in a satisfactory way.

_____ Gathers information from more than one source

_____ Organizes information to demonstrate a reasonable understanding of how germs are spread and how people can stop the spread of germs

_____ Works alone with initiative or works cooperatively with others much of the time

_____ Communicates ideas in a reasonably clear and effective way through a bulletin board display

_____ Demonstrates some commitment to stop the spread of germs

Level 1
The student does not fulfill the purpose of the project.

_____ Gathers insufficient information or uses only one source

_____ Fails to organize information to demonstrate a reasonable understanding of how germs are spread and how people can stop the spread of germs

_____ Lacks initiative when working alone or fails to work cooperatively

_____ Has difficulty communicating clear, complete ideas through a bulletin board display

_____ Demonstrates little commitment to stop the spread of germs

Student's overall score _____

Teacher comments:

Medicines and Other Drugs

Chapter 6 Test

Write the letter of the correct term in the space.

a. drug	d. side effects
b. over-the-counter medicine	e. caffeine
c. prescription medicine	

Dana was feeling ill, so her mother took her to see Doctor Chu. Doctor Chu examined Dana and said she needed medicines to help her get well. He wrote an order for a **1.** ____ and asked Dana's mom to also buy a bottle of **2.** ____ at the pharmacy. Doctor Chu told Dana not to drink anything that has **3.** ____ in it, such as some sodas. He said that caffeine is a **4.** ____ that can interact with the medicines and could cause some **5.** ____ .

Write *T* or *F* to show if the sentence is true or false.

_____ **6.** A drug is something other than food that changes how the body works.

_____ **7.** Caffeine makes people feel more awake.

_____ **8.** Drugs can never be harmful.

_____ **9.** Many household products give off dangerous fumes.

_____ **10.** "High" is a common way of describing people who take medicine ordered by a doctor.

_____ **11.** Over-the-counter medicines cannot be bought without an order from a doctor.

_____ **12.** OTC medicines are for minor health problems like sore throats, colds, and headaches.

_____ **13.** It is not important for adults to follow the directions on OTC medicines.

_____ **14.** A prescription medicine is a medicine that must be ordered by a doctor.

_____ **15.** The order a doctor writes for a medicine is called a pharmacist.

Name _____ Date _____

Choose the sentences below that are good safety rules for using medicines. Write their letters on the lines.

a. Only an adult should give you medicine.

b. It's OK to take the labels off medicines.

c. Never take someone else's prescription medicine.

d. Always follow the directions on a medicine.

e. Children should take medicines on their own.

f. Keep medicines away from small children.

g. Keep medicines on high shelves or in locked cabinets.

_____16.

_____17.

_____18.

_____19.

_____20.

21. List some ways to avoid taking in caffeine.

_____

_____

_____

22. Name three harmful reactions a person could have from inhaling fumes from dangerous products.

_____

_____

_____

23. Lexie's older brother uses marijuana and cocaine. What could Lexie tell her brother about these two dangerous drugs that might get him to stop using them?

_____

_____

_____

_____

_____

24. Kevin doesn't want to take illegal drugs. What does Kevin know about illegal drugs that might make him feel this way?

_____

_____

_____

_____

Some older kids at Melissa's school use drugs.
Today they will ask Melissa to use drugs. Draw
two ways Melissa can say *no* to drugs.

25.

26.

Harcourt Brace School Publishers

Name _____ Date _____

Chapter Project Evaluation Sheet (Teacher)

Rubric for Evaluating Student Performance on the Chapter 6 Project

Project: Make posters
Purpose: To gather and organize information about drugs and medicines; to develop work skills; to use what is learned from the project in everyday life

Use the indicators below to help you determine the student's overall score.

Level 3
The student fulfills the purpose of the project in an exemplary way.

_____ Gathers information from a variety of sources

_____ Organizes information to demonstrate a thorough understanding of the positive and negative effects of drugs

_____ Works alone with initiative or works cooperatively with others

_____ Communicates ideas clearly and effectively through posters

_____ Demonstrates strong commitment to applying the content of the posters to everyday life

Level 2

The student fulfills the purpose of the project in a satisfactory way.

_____ Gathers information from more than one source

_____ Organizes information to demonstrate a reasonable understanding of the positive and negative effects of drugs

_____ Works alone with initiative or works cooperatively with others much of the time

_____ Communicates ideas in a reasonably clear and effective way through posters

_____ Demonstrates some commitment to applying the content of the posters to everyday life

Level 1

The student does not fulfill the purpose of the project.

_____ Gathers insufficient information or uses only one source

_____ Fails to organize information to demonstrate a reasonable understanding of the positive and negative effects of drugs

_____ Lacks initiative when working alone or fails to work cooperatively

_____ Has difficulty communicating clear, complete ideas through posters

_____ Demonstrates little commitment to applying the content of the posters to everyday life

Student's overall score _____

Teacher comments

Name _____ Date _____

Avoiding Alcohol and Tobacco

Write *T* or *F* to show if the sentence is true or false.

_____ **1.** Both tobacco and alcohol are drugs.

_____ **2.** A cigarette is the only type of tobacco product that has nicotine.

_____ **3.** Nicotine makes users want more tobacco.

_____ **4.** Alcohol causes changes in a person's body.

_____ **5.** Some people who use alcohol can't stop using it.

Use the words below to finish the stories.

addiction	smokeless tobacco	tar
environmental tobacco smoke	chewing tobacco	cancer

6. Tara's uncle smokes cigarettes. He has trouble breathing when he works hard because his lungs are coated with a dark, sticky substance called

_____.

7. Peter knows that using tobacco can cause a disease called

_____.

8. The Chu family does not allow people to smoke in their home. They know that being in a room full of cigarette smoke can be harmful. This

kind of smoke is called _____

_____.

9. Tobacco is not always smoked. Sometimes it is chewed. Mr. McGuire doesn't smoke or chew tobacco. He puts pinches of tobacco between his cheek and gum. This kind of tobacco is called

_____.

10. Rebecca's oldest brother smokes cigarettes. He wants to stop but it is

hard. His _____ to nicotine keeps him smoking.

Harcourt Brace School Publishers

Complete the diagram below by telling how alcohol can harm the parts of the body shown. The first one is done for you.

Brain Alcohol affects speech. It slows down how a person sees and moves. It can make the brain stop working, causing death.

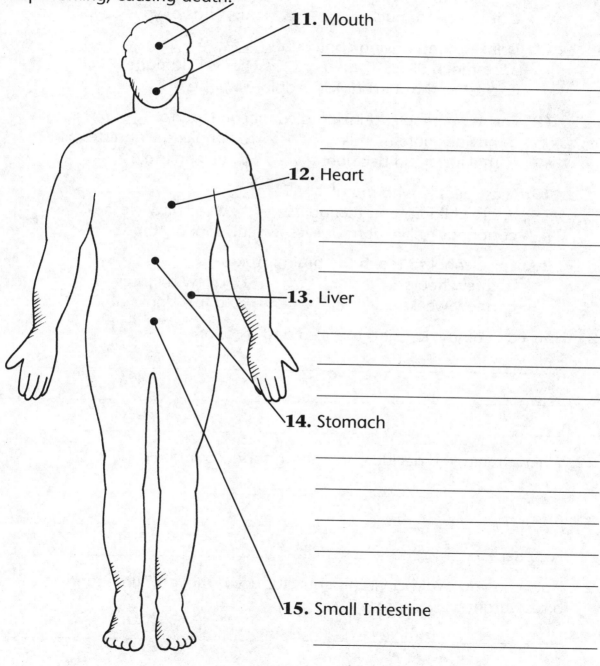

11. Mouth

_____

_____

_____

_____

12. Heart

_____

_____

_____

13. Liver

_____

_____

_____

_____

14. Stomach

_____

_____

_____

_____

15. Small Intestine

_____

_____

Name _____ Date _____

Write the letter of the best answer on the line at the left.

_____ **16.** One reason it is against the law for children to buy or drink alcohol is _____.
    a. its taste is not liked by children
    b. it prevents normal brain and body growth
    c. it costs too much
    d. it has always been illegal

_____ **17.** Drinking and driving can cause _____.
    a. stomach ulcers
    b. liver damage
    c. crashes that hurt or kill people
    d. fights

_____ **18.** For some people, drinking alcohol can lead to _____.
    a. having more friends
    b. smoking cigarettes
    c. making good decisions
    d. alcoholism

_____ **19.** Most people who are alcoholics _____.
    a. are children and teenagers
    b. wear dirty clothes
    c. appear to live normal lives
    d. appear to be sad

_____ **20.** For alcohol to reach the brain it takes _____.
    a. a few hours
    b. a few minutes
    c. a few weeks
    d. a few drinks

21. How can you avoid using tobacco and alcohol?

_____

_____

_____

22. When should you decide about using tobacco and alcohol?

_____

_____

_____

23. How can you avoid environmental tobacco smoke when eating at a restaurant?

_____

_____

_____

Chapter Project Evaluation Sheet (Teacher)

**Rubric for Evaluating Student Performance
on the Chapter 7 Project**

Project: Make a life-sized model of the body
Purpose: To gather and organize information to show the effects of alcohol and tobacco
on the body; to develop work skills; to use what is learned in everyday life

Use the indicators below to help you determine the student's overall score.

Level 3
The student fulfills the purpose of the project in an exemplary way.

_____ Gathers information from a variety of sources

_____ Organizes information to demonstrate a thorough understanding of the effects of
alcohol or tobacco on the body

_____ Works alone with initiative or works cooperatively with others

_____ Communicates ideas clearly and effectively through a life-sized body model

_____ Demonstrates strong ability to apply the information in the life-sized body model to
a personal commitment to avoid drinking alcohol and avoid using tobacco

Level 2
The student fulfills the purpose of the project in a satisfactory way.

_____ Gathers information from more than one source

_____ Organizes information to demonstrate a reasonable understanding of the effects of
alcohol or tobacco on the body

_____ Works alone with initiative or works cooperatively with others much of the time

_____ Communicates ideas reasonably, clearly, and effectively through a life-sized model

_____ Demonstrates some ability to apply the information in the life-sized body model to
a personal commitment to avoid drinking alcohol and avoid using tobacco

Level 1
The student does not fulfill the purpose of the project.

_____ Gathers insufficient information or uses only one source

_____ Fails to organize information to demonstrate adequate understanding of the effects
of alcohol or tobacco on the body

_____ Lacks initiative when working alone or fails to work cooperatively

_____ Has difficulty communicating clear, complete ideas through a life-sized body model

_____ Demonstrates little ability to apply the information in the life-sized body model to a
personal commitment to avoid drinking alcohol and avoid using tobacco

Student's overall score _____
Teacher comments:

Keeping Safe

Write *T* or *F* to show if the statement is true or false.

_____ **1.** Family members have a responsibility to protect you.

_____ **2.** You have no duty to help protect yourself.

_____ **3.** Safety rules are rules that can be dangerous.

_____ **4.** An injury is harm done to a person's body.

_____ **5.** A hazard is a rule that helps protect you from injury.

_____ **6.** A limit is a point at which you must stop.

_____ **7.** A passenger is someone riding in a car or bus.

_____ **8.** The safest place for children in a car is in the front seat.

_____ **9.** It's safe to walk on the road.

_____ **10.** Crossing a street in the middle of the block is as safe as crossing at a corner.

11. Cross out the one thing you should *never* do when a stranger approaches you.

Ignore him or her.

Go in a car with him or her.

Leave the area.

Run away and yell, "I don't know you."

12. Cross out the person below who would *not* be thought of as a trusted adult.

a grandparent

a teacher

a good neighbor

a police officer

a security guard

a stranger on the street

13. Circle the safety rules you *could* follow when faced with a bully.

Ignore mean remarks.

Don't talk back or fight.

Yell something mean back at the person.

Get help if the bully follows you.

Stay with others.

Choose friends who stay away from bullies.

Keep running if the bully follows you.

14. Cross out the sentences below that are *not* emergencies.

Your house is on fire.

Your mother has fallen and is injured.

Someone is knocking on your front door.

The wind has blown over your patio furniture.

Your younger brother has swallowed poison.

A storm has blown off part of your roof.

15. Draw a picture of yourself escaping a fire. Be sure that your picture shows you practicing something that you learned about safely escaping a fire.

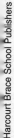

Harcourt Brace School Publishers

Name _____ Date _____

Write the letter of the best answer on the line in
front of the sentence.

_____ 16. When unplugging a lamp, hold the _____ .
     a. cord   **b.** plug   **c.** lamp   **d.** shade

_____ 17. Never plug in or turn on electrical things when you have _____ .
     a. wet hands   **b.** eyeglasses on
     c. dry hands   **d.** a book in your hand

_____ 18. A substance that causes illness or death when it gets into the
     body is called a _____ .
     a. medicine   **b.** cover
     c. home product   **d.** poison

_____ 19. Clothing or equipment worn to protect players from injury is
     called _____ .
     a. safety net   **b.** safety belt
     c. safety guard   **d.** safety gear

_____ 20. The most important safety gear to wear while bicycling _____ .
     a. is a mouth guard   **b.** are wrist guards
     c. is a helmet   **d.** are elbow pads

_____ 21. When you buy a helmet, you should look for _____ .
     a. the price tag   **b.** a helmet that fits loosely
     c. your favorite color   **d.** a hard shell and an approval
                                     sticker

_____ 22. If someone has been poisoned, call _____ .
     a. the Poison Control Center   **b.** 911
     c. your neighbor   **d.** your local police

_____ 23. If someone is very ill and there is no adult to tell, call _____ .
     a. 911   **b.** the Poison Control Center
     c. your local police   **d.** your teacher

_____ 24. Caring for small injuries is called _____ .
     a. dangerous   **b.** first aid
     c. an emergency   **d.** an antiseptic

_____ 25. The first thing you should do about an injury is _____ .
     a. call 911   **b.** call the Poison Control Center
     c. tell an adult   **d.** tell a friend

Chapter Project Evaluation Sheet (Teacher)

Rubric for Evaluating Student Performance on the Chapter 8 Project

Project: Make a safety collage

Purpose: To gather and organize information to make a collage showing how you can stay safe at home, at school, and at play; to develop work skills; to use what is learned from the project in everyday life

Use the indicators below to help you determine the student's overall score.

Level 3
The student fulfills the purpose of the project in an exemplary way.

_____ Gathers information from a variety of sources

_____ Organizes information to demonstrate thorough understanding of safety at home, school, and play

_____ Works alone with initiative or works cooperatively with others

_____ Communicates ideas clearly and effectively through a collage

_____ Demonstrates strong ability to apply the information in the collage to a personal commitment to practicing safety

Level 2
The student fulfills the purpose of the project in a satisfactory way.

_____ Gathers information from more than one source

_____ Organizes information to demonstrate reasonable understanding of safety at home, school, and play

_____ Works alone with initiative or works cooperatively with others most of the time

_____ Communicates ideas reasonably well through a collage

_____ Demonstrates some ability to apply the information in the collage to a personal commitment to practicing safety

Level 1
The student does not fulfill the purpose of the project.

_____ Gathers insufficient information or uses only one source

_____ Fails to organize information to demonstrate reasonable understanding of safety at home, school, and play

_____ Lacks initiative when working alone or fails to work cooperatively with others

_____ Has difficulty communicating clear, complete ideas through a collage

_____ Demonstrates little ability to apply the information in the collage to a personal commitment to practicing safety

Student's overall score _____

Teacher comments:

Health in the Community

Match the words below with the sentences that best give their meanings. Write the letter of the word on the line at the left.

a. community	**c.** hospital	**e.** registered nurse
b. health department	**d.** clinic	

_____ **1.** This is a place where badly hurt or very ill people get medical treatment.

_____ **2.** This is a place where people live, work, play, and go to school.

_____ **3.** This health-care worker helps doctors during treatments and checkups. He or she gives medicine and cares for people who are ill or hurt.

_____ **4.** This group of health-care workers works for the government and serves a community.

_____ **5.** This is another place where people can get health care. Sometimes the cost is low or even free.

Complete the chart. Write one example of each.

Kind of Pollution	Examples
6. air	
7. noise	
8. water	

9. Name three things that are part of your environment.

_____

_____

_____

10. How does a pollution control technician help reduce air pollution?

_____

_____

_____

Write *T* or *F* to show if the sentence is true or false.

_____**11.** Health department workers are also called public health workers.

_____**12.** Public health officers keep records of diseases that can spread.

_____**13.** Surgeons are doctors who do operations.

_____**14.** Doctors and nurses in a clinic treat people who are very sick or badly hurt.

_____**15.** Pollution is dirt and harmful materials in the air, water, or land.

_____**16.** People never cause air pollution.

_____**17.** Many cities burn trash outside.

_____**18.** Disturbing or harmful sounds made by human activities cause noise pollution.

_____**19.** Pollution control technicians check factories to make sure workers are not harmed by unsafe noise levels.

_____**20.** Groundwater is the water that comes from lakes and rivers.

Name _____ Date _____

21. Elena doesn't understand why littering can hurt some ocean animals. How would you explain to Elena why she shouldn't litter?

_____

_____

_____

_____

Many objects in our environment can be reused or recycled, or their use can be reduced. Complete the chart by naming one way each object can be reduced, reused, or recycled.

Objects	Reduce, Reuse, Recycle
22. newspapers	
23. plastic bottles	
24. clothes	
25. paper	

Chapter Project Evaluation Sheet (Teacher)

Rubric for Evaluating Student Performance on the Chapter 9 Project

Project: Plan a site for gathering reusable materials

Purpose: To gather and organize information to make a plan for reusing materials in the classroom; to develop work skills; to use what is learned in everyday life

Use the indicators below to help you determine the student's overall score.

Level 3
The student fulfills the purpose of the project in an exemplary way.

_____ Gathers information from a variety of sources

_____ Organizes information to demonstrate thorough understanding of a plan for reusing materials in the classroom

_____ Works alone with initiative or works cooperatively with others

_____ Communicates ideas clearly and effectively through a plan for reusing materials

_____ Demonstrates strong ability to apply the information in the plan to a personal commitment to reusing classroom materials

Level 2
The student fulfills the purpose of the project in a satisfactory way.

_____ Gathers information from more than one source

_____ Organizes information to demonstrate reasonable understanding of a plan for reusing materials in the classroom

_____ Works alone with initiative or works cooperatively with others most of the time

_____ Communicates ideas reasonably well through a plan for reusing materials

_____ Demonstrates some ability to apply the information in the plan to a personal commitment to reusing classroom materials

Level 1
The student does not fulfill the purpose of the project.

_____ Gathers insufficient information or uses only one source

_____ Fails to organize information to demonstrate reasonable understanding of a plan for reusing materials in the classroom

_____ Lacks initiative when working alone or fails to works cooperatively with others

_____ Has difficulty communicating clear, complete ideas through a plan for reusing materials

_____ Demonstrates little ability to apply the information in the plan to a personal commitment to reusing classroom materials

Student's overall score _____

Teacher comments:

Chapter 1 Test • About Myself and Others

page 18
1. T
2. F
3. T
4. T
5. F
6. T
7. F
8. F
9. T
10. T
11. anger
12. fear

page 19
13. stress
14. grief
15. Possible answers: when you have trouble sleeping; when you are afraid to go to school; when something makes you feel uncomfortable and scared; when someone touches you in a way you don't like.
16. Possible answers: plan your time wisely; set goals you can reach; get some exercise; take time to have fun.
17. Possible answers: stop what you are doing; count to ten to cool down; think about what is happening; take action; use "I-messages."
18. Drawing should show words or actions, as well as body language, to display communication.
19. Drawing should show student saying or doing something that shows that he or she shares the same feelings as the person who is experiencing a hardship or other trouble.

page 20
20. a
21. c
22. b
23. a
24. d
25. Possible answers: I feel bad when you say those words to me; I feel angry when you talk to me like that; I feel hurt when you use those words.

Chapter 2 Test • Me and My Family

page 22

1. F
2. T
3. T
4. F
5. F
6. T
7. T
8. T
9. F
10. T
11. changes
12. divorce
13. sibling
14. communicate
15. family

page 23

16. a
17. c
18. d
19. b
20. Possible answers: I can now do many things for myself; I can walk and talk and sit up; I have grown much larger; I can read and write.
21. b
22. d
23. a
24. c
25. c

page 24

26. Possible answers: everyone grows at his or her own rate; his body is growing just as it should; growth spurts happen to children at different ages; he is unique—not even his twin is exactly like him.
27. Possible answers; eat healthful foods, get regular checkups, get plenty of rest, be vaccinated against disease, keep your body clean, exercise.
28. Sue Ann should tell the person to stop and then tell a trusted adult about what is happening.
29. Comparing myself to others might make me feel as if I am not growing fast enough or big enough; I might feel something is wrong with me.
30. blood, heart, and blood vessels

Chapter 3 Test • Keeping My Body Fit

page 26
1. T
2. F
3. T
4. T
5. T
6. F
7. T
8. F
9. F
10. T
11. fluoride
12. dental floss
13. plaque
14. mouth guard
15. cavity

page 27
16. outer ear
17. ear canal
18. middle ear
19. inner ear
20. eardrum
21. Wear a helmet.
22. He should sit or stand up straight and tip his head forward, while pinching his nose.
23. b
24. d

page 28
25. a
26. Kenny forgot to warm up his muscles.
27. Marta should have stopped running and told her teacher.
28. They forgot to cool down their muscles.
29. The physical therapist will help her regain movement and strength in her arm.
30. Louis's dad put ice on the injured knee.

Chapter 4 Test • Food for a Healthy Body

page 30
1. c
2. a
3. b
4. d
5. c
6. T
7. T
8. F
9. F
10. T
11. F
12. T
13. T
14. F
15. F

page 31
16. milk, yogurt, and cheese group
17. meat, poultry, eggs, and nuts group
18. vegetable group
19. fruit group
20. bread, cereal, rice, and pasta group
21. bread, cereal, rice, and pasta group
22. fats, oils, and sweets group
23. water
24. a balanced diet
25. No. We should space our meals so that our bodies have the energy and nutrients they need all day long.

page 32
26. oranges, apples, bagels, cheese, raisins, orange juice, milk
27. middle label
28. a large can of orange juice
29. Store Brand Whole Wheat Crackers
30. a large bag of pretzels

Chapter 5 Test • Preventing Disease

page 34

1. g
2. e
3. a
4. j
5. d
6. h
7. i
8. f
9. b
10. c

page 35

11. T
12. F
13. F
14. T
15. F
16. F
17. T
18. T
19. F
20. F
21. Possible answers: The doctor can prescribe medicine; the doctor can give her shots.
22. Possible answers: Kenny's allergies might be worse than usual; he might have exercised too hard; he might have a disease.
23. She can follow a special diet; she can take medicine.

page 36

24. Menu #1
25. Exercise makes your muscles, heart, and lungs stronger. Exercise helps you manage stress.

Harcourt Brace School Publishers

Chapter 6 Test • Medicines and Other Drugs

page 38

1. c
2. b
3. e
4. a
5. d
6. T
7. T
8. F
9. T
10. F
11. F
12. T
13. F
14. T
15. F

page 39

16. a
17. c
18. d
19. f
20. g
21. Know which foods and drinks have caffeine. Do not eat chocolate. Drink soft drinks that do not contain caffeine.
22. Sample answers: nosebleed, confusion, hearing loss, upset stomach, violent behavior, headache, sneezing, coughing, slowed breathing rate, death.

page 40

23. Sample answers: These drugs can speed up the heart; make it hard for the body to fight infections; cause cancer; make users feel nervous, sad, confused, angry, or tired; lead to brain or lung damage; make users need more and more of the drugs.
24. Kevin knows that a person can go to jail for using illegal drugs. He also knows that illegal drugs can change the way the brain works so a person cannot think well. Drugs also can cause illness or death.
25-26. Students' art might show Melissa saying, "No thanks," and walking away; saying, "I want to have fun, not hurt my body"; or saying, "I can have fun without drugs."

Chapter 7 Test • Avoiding Alcohol and Tobacco

page 42
1. T
2. F
3. T
4. T
5. T
6. tar
7. cancer
8. environmental tobacco smoke
9. smokeless tobacco
10. addiction

page 43
11. Alcohol can cause a tingling in the mouth. It can make the mouth, tongue, and food tube sore.
12. Alcohol makes the heart beat faster. It makes blood pressure go up.
13. Alcohol can stay in the liver causing liver damage.
14. Alcohol can cause an upset stomach. Regular, heavy drinking can cause holes, or ulcers, in the stomach.
15. Alcohol can destroy chemicals that digest food.

page 44
16. b
17. c
18. d
19. c
20. b
21. Possible answers: say *no* when offered either tobacco or alcohol, stay away from places where young people use them, find friends who don't use these products.
22. Possible answer: Decide ahead of time, before you are offered these products.
23. Possible answer: Ask to sit in a non-smoking section.

Chapter 8 Test • Keeping Safe

page 46
1. T
2. F
3. F
4. T
5. F
6. T
7. T
8. F
9. F
10. F
11. Go in a car with him or her.
12. a stranger on the street

page 47
13. Ignore mean remarks.
    Don't talk back or fight.
    Get help if the bully follows you.
    Stay with others.
    Choose friends who stay away from bullies.
14. Someone is knocking on your front door.
    The wind has blown over your patio furniture.
15. The picture should show one of the following: child crawling out of a room; warning others; following an escape route; meeting family outside; calling 911 or the fire department; stop, drop, roll.

page 48
16. b
17. a
18. d
19. d
20. c
21. d
22. a
23. a
24. b
25. c

Chapter 9 Test • Health in the Community

page 50
 1. c
 2. a
 3. e
 4. b
 5. d
Possible answers are shown.
 6. materials from factories, cars, trucks, and buses; tobacco smoke
 7. vacuum cleaners; jackhammers; loud radios
 8. motor oil from cars; chemicals from factories and farms; salt used on icy highways; lawn chemicals

page 51
 9. Accept all reasonable answers.
 10. He or she tests water, air, or soil for harmful substances.
 11. T
 12. T
 13. T
 14. F
 15. T
 16. F
 17. F
 18. T
 19. T
 20. F

page 52
 21. Some ocean animals, such as sea turtles, die because they eat balloons or plastic bags in the water. They mistake them for jellyfish, their favorite food.
 22. can be recycled in most communities
 23. can be recycled, some can be reused, their use can be reduced by buying beverages in glass bottles
 24. can be reused by giving them to someone smaller when you outgrow them
 25. use glasses instead of paper cups, borrow library books instead of buying books, reuse paper as scrap paper